Spiralize!

TRANSFORM FRUITS AND VEGETABLES FROM ORDINARY TO EXTRAORDINARY

Beverly Lynn Bennett

books
Alive

Summertown
TENNESSEE

CONTENTS

RECIPES

3

ACKNOWLEDGMENTS

I'd like to express my heartfelt appreciation to several people who helped make this book possible: Cynthia and Bob Holzapfel, my talented editor Jo Stepaniak, and the rest of the staff at Book Publishing Company, which publishes and produces so many fantastic vegan and vegetarian lifestyle books and cookbooks. I would also like to thank my family and friends for their love and support, especially my husband, Ray Sammartano, and my feline companion, Luna, for all their help during the recipe testing and writing of this book. And last but not least, to my fellow vegans, thank you for doing all that you can to spread the vegan message and for choosing to improve your lives and the lives of our fellow creatures who share this planet with us.

INTRODUCTION

What's the coolest craze to hit the culinary world? Spiralizing! No doubt you've seen the latest kitchen gadgets known as spiralizers, which are sold in stores, online, and via TV ads. With just a few turns of a hand crank or a twist of the wrist, a spiralizer (the umbrella term that encompasses both spiralizers and spiral slicers) can quickly and easily turn your favorite fruits and vegetables into pastalike noodles of various shapes and sizes.

For decades, raw food enthusiasts and chefs have been using spiralizers to create nutritious, colorful garnishes and captivating components for use in salads, soups, sandwiches, side dishes, and entrées, and now you can too! Spiralizers are simple to use and great for preparing healthy and delicious vegetable-based meals in a fraction of the time it would take to cut everything by hand. These practical gadgets are especially convenient for people with minimal knife skills because they're so simple to operate. Even cooks with limited culinary experience can easily add more variety to meals just by incorporating spiralized foods. You'll have great fun reinventing your favorite recipes by substituting spiralized vegetables for rice or pasta. As a bonus, spiralizing enhances the visual appeal of vegetables and fruits, so you'll no doubt dazzle your friends and family with your impressive creations.

ADVANTAGES OF SPIRALIZING

We all know that fruits and vegetables are nutritional powerhouses packed with the vitamins, minerals, antioxidants, and other nutrients that our bodies need to function optimally. Spiralizing actually makes it a joy to get more of these important healthy foods into our diets. A spiralizer is the ideal device for health-conscious people who already eat with an eye toward good nutrition, as well as for those who want to make positive dietary changes by incorporating more fruits and vegetables into their daily meals. Spiralizing is also a terrific technique for enticing finicky eaters to consume more health-promoting foods by making them more fun and appealing.

Pasta and rice made from spiralized vegetables are perfect for people who follow a gluten-free, low-carb, paleo, or raw food diet and those who are watching their weight or trying to lose a few pounds. That's because pastas made from fresh vegetables have fewer calories and carbohydrates than grain-based pastas. They also contain more fiber than conventional pasta, and fiber helps us feel fuller longer and improves digestion and regularity. In addition, fruits and vegetables have a high water content, and that's valuable for keeping us hydrated and aids the body's natural detoxification process. As a bonus, you can indulge as much as you like in pastas made from vegetables because they're packed with great nutrition.

Spiralizers are hand-operated gadgets and need no electricity or batteries to operate. This makes them extremely portable, and they can be used almost anywhere and under almost any circumstances. People with busy schedules will appreciate both how easy and convenient it is to use spiralizers and how these uncomplicated devices can minimize the time it takes to prep and cook meals.

A spiralizer can safely be operated by anyone, even an older child with proper supervision. Many young people enjoy helping out in the kitchen, and they'll have a blast making creative spiralized dishes. Just watch their awe and delight as they turn a humble zucchini into a giant pile of spaghetti! Plus, kids tend to eat more of a meal when it's one they've helped to prepare, and what parent wouldn't appreciate that?

DIFFERENT TYPES OF SPIRALIZERS

There are several different styles of spiralizers, and they're available in various shapes, sizes, colors, and price ranges. Depending on the type and brand, they each have slightly different features and capabilities. What they all have in common, however, are sharp, stainless steel cutting blades, which either have a straight edge, comblike teeth, or triangle-shaped cutouts. The number of teeth and amount of space between them, or the smaller the size of the triangle cutouts, will determine the width and thickness of the cut that can be achieved.

Some spiralizers come with a range of blades, and there will no doubt be one that you can use to spiralize your favorite fruits or vegetables into various pasta shapes, such as angel hair, thin spaghetti, thick spaghetti, flat linguine, or fettuccine. But you're not limited to just replicating pasta, as you can also use a knife or the pulse setting of a food processor to cut the spiralized strands into rice-sized pieces for use in recipes that are commonly made with rice. Depending on the blades included with your device, you might also be able to cut ribbons, circular slices, half-moons, and thin or thick shreds.

Based on how the device operates, in conjunction with the position of the cutting blade, spiralizers can be classified into three basic styles: horizontal tri-blade spiralizer, vertical spiral slicer, and handheld hourglass spiral slicer. Following is a brief description of the three styles and how they operate, along with brand-name examples of each type:

HORIZONTAL TRI-BLADE SPIRALIZER (such as Paderno). This type of spiralizer is commonly referred to as a tri-blade because it has three interchangeable blades: a shredder (fine shredder) that makes thin spaghetti-like noodles; a chipper (coarse shredder) that makes thick spaghetti, linguine, fettuccine, or udon noodles; and a straight blade (spiral shredder) that makes wide, flat ribbons, pappardelle, or lasagna-shaped noodles, depending on the width of the vegetable or fruit being used. The straight blade can also be used to shred vegetables, such as cabbage, for use in slaws, salads, and other dishes. Some brands are also available in a four-blade version, which is capable of making very fine angel hair noodles.

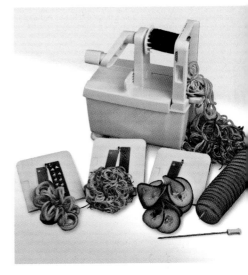

A tri-blade spiralizer consists of three main parts: the cutting blades, the crank handle, and the base. Some models have a blade storage area in the base. The base also has suction cups on the bottom to help securely anchor the spiralizer to a dry countertop or cutting board during use. To use the device, a vegetable or fruit is centered on the circular corer on the blade plate of the machine, then anchored in place by pressing the spikes in the crank handle into the opposite end. By turning the crank handle clockwise with one hand while simultaneously pushing forward on the lever handle with the other hand, the item is guided toward the cutting blade and cut into the desired shape.

Tri-blade spiralizers take up more storage space in a cabinet or on the counter than other types of spiralizers. However, their sturdiness and bigger size makes it easier to spiralize a wider assortment of vegetables and fruits, especially ones that are dense or large, and to quickly produce a substantial amount of pasta. This type of spiralizer also makes longer and thicker noodles or ribbons, since it can handle produce that is up to ten inches long and seven inches in diameter. In addition, tri-blade spiralizers are safer to use than handheld hourglass spiral slicers, as fingers remain far from the cutting blades during use.

VERTICAL SPIRAL SLICER (such as GEFU Spiralfix or Saladacco). Most models of vertical spiral slicers have two or more blade options. They also have several parts: a cutting table that contains the cutting blades and their adjustment lever, a spiked holder plate, and a crank handle. Some models also include a transparent protective cover and a collection container for the spiralized fruit or vegetable. It's operated by turning the crank handle clockwise while pushing downward with the palm of your hand, which in turn pushes the food against the cutting blade, and the spiralized item is dropped below.

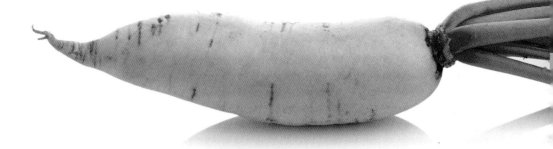

A vertical spiral slicer works best with short, slender vegetables and fruits, no more than three and a half inches in length and at least one inch in diameter. As a result, it makes shorter, thinner, and finer-shaped noodles and ribbons from intact cut pieces of produce. Vertically scored pieces can be cut into thin strips, thin rounds, or half-moons. This type of spiralizer works well for beets, carrots, cucumbers, daikon radishes and other radishes, onions, potatoes, sweet potatoes, turnips, yellow squash, and zucchini. It works especially well with firmer vegetables, such as root vegetables, but it doesn't do well with soft vegetables, such as tomatoes.

HANDHELD HOURGLASS SPIRAL SLICER (such as Brieftons NextGen or Veggetti). Most models of this type of spiral slicer have two or more blade options. They have an hourglass shape, with two funnel-shaped openings that contain the cutting blades and a handle for gripping in the middle. Handheld hourglass spiral slicers are operated much like a pencil sharpener: a vegetable (or fruit) is inserted into one of the openings, and as you turn the vegetable against the cutting blade, it peels off into thin or thick spaghetti, linguine, or ribbon strands. Some brands come with a spiked grip cap, or safety holder, for working with the last few inches of a vegetable. Alternatively, you can pierce the end of the vegetable with a fork for use in a similar manner. Handheld hourglass spiral slicers make shorter noodles and are good for producing small quantities. They are the smallest of the spiral slicers, which makes them ideal for use when traveling.

A handheld hourglass spiral slicer works best with vegetables that are long and slender or cone-shaped. The vegetable must not be wider than the inside of the spiral slicer (typically under three inches) or they'll need to be cut in half lengthwise. The process will go more smoothly and you'll have less waste if you spiralize the fatter end of the vegetable first and hold on to the stem or thinner end of the vegetable. This type of spiralizer works well with carrots, cucumbers, daikon radishes, parsnips and similar root vegetables, yellow squash, and zucchini. It doesn't work well with irregularly shaped or overly large vegetables, eggplants, or apples and other fruits.

SELECTING FRUITS AND VEGETABLES FOR SPIRALIZING

Success with spiralizing certain vegetables and fruits greatly depends on the type of spiralizer you use. Although some spiralizers can be used for cabbages and bell peppers, in general, spiralizing works best for firmer vegetables, such as the following:

beets	fennel	rutabagas
carrots	jicama	sweet potatoes
celeriac	kohlrabi	turnips and similar
cucumbers	onions	root vegetables
daikon radishes and other radishes	parsnips	winter squash
	potatoes	yellow squash
		zucchini

A tri-blade spiralizer and some models of spiral slicers can also be used to spiralize several varieties of firm fruits, including apples, papayas, pears, plantains, and similar fruits. With the exception of pears, choose fruit that is fully ripe. You may run into problems trying to spiralize vegetables and fruits that are overly soft, small, or hollow inside.

In general, choose vegetables that feel firm and have few or no seeds, and select ones that are relatively straight rather than bent, curved, or irregularly shaped. For example, with cucumbers, you'll have the best outcome with the English variety, as they are thinner and tend to have fewer and smaller seeds than standard cucumbers. As a general rule of thumb, depending on the type and model of spiralizer you're using, choose produce that is medium to large and at least one or more inches wide.

Whenever possible, opt for organically grown produce, especially if you want to leave the skins on; otherwise, peel the items prior to spiralizing them. Thoroughly wash and pat dry the produce before spiralizing it. In most instances, it's a good idea to cut off both ends of the vegetable or fruit before spiralizing it so the edges are flat, and position the item as straight as possible against the cutting blade. Feel free to experiment with spiralizing various kinds of vegetables and fruits to see which ones work best with the type of spiralizer you have.

CLEANING AND SAFETY TIPS

Before using a spiralizer for the first time, read the instruction manual that came with it to familiarize yourself with how to assemble, use, clean, and care for it properly, along with any safety precautions. While tri-blade spiralizers and spiral slicers can differ greatly with regard to usage and design, they all have a lot in common in terms of composition. The majority of spiralizer parts are made of sturdy plastic, and their cutting blades are made of stainless steel. Be aware that the cutting blades are razor sharp and should be handled with care; never touch them with your fingers. If the cutting blade becomes clogged while you're spiralizing, carefully use a fork, knife, chopstick, or brush to scrape away any debris, or rinse the blade under running water.

Most spiralizers can be disassembled for easier cleaning. Rinse the parts under running water, then use a toothbrush or dishwashing brush (preferably one with a long handle), along with soap and hot water, to scrub the cutting blades and parts clean. After cleaning the device, shake off any excess water to help the various parts air-dry faster. Alternatively, use a thick towel to carefully pat the blades dry to help avoid rust or tarnishing. Some spiralizers are dishwasher safe. Regularly spiralizing certain vegetables that contain a lot of natural pigment, such as carrots and beets, might cause some of the plastic parts to become stained. Prompt cleaning, however, will remove most staining. Tough stains can be removed by rubbing them with a towel or cotton swab dipped in rubbing alcohol, vinegar, or lemon juice.

SPIRALIZING TIPS

As with most things, practice makes perfect, and the same can be said of spiralizing. The more you use your spiralizer, the better your results will be and the more your spiralized pieces will be uniform in shape and length. With a little luck, you might even be able to achieve one long continuous noodle, which is quite an amazing spectacle! While long noodles may look impressive, they can be a bit difficult to serve and eat without making a mess, which is why I suggest using a knife to cut them into shorter lengths before using them in recipes.

It's wise to spiralize vegetables just before making a recipe so they'll be as fresh as possible. However, if you prefer to prep a lot of different types of vegetables at one time, you can spiralize larger batches for multiple recipes and store them in airtight containers or ziplock bags lined with paper towels; they'll keep in the refrigerator for two to three days.

I don't recommend freezing spiralized vegetables, as they tend to become mushy when thawed. Fruits should always be spiralized just before using.

Many vegetables have a very high water content, especially those with a lot of seeds, such as cucumbers, yellow squash, and zucchini. To avoid having soggy noodles, put them between two paper towels and pat gently to remove excess moisture. Also, to reduce the chances of a finished dish getting too watery, use a dressing or sauce with a slightly thicker consistency than you would normally use for a grain-based pasta dish, and toss the noodles with the dressing or sauce just before serving. I recommend using a larger amount of spiralized pasta and a lesser amount of dressing or sauce. I've found that using twice as much spiralized pasta as dressing or sauce works well for most dishes.

No matter which type of spiralizer you use, you will never be able to spiralize an entire vegetable or fruit; there will always be a small portion left over. There are several options for using up these bits and pieces. Naturally, you could just eat, compost, or discard them, but you could also save them in a ziplock bag or airtight container in your freezer or refrigerator and use them for making soups, stews, smoothies, or other recipes. I usually just finely chop or slice the leftover pieces and add them to the recipe along with the spiralized items.

Other than potatoes, all spiralized fruits and vegetables can be eaten raw, and doing so will retain more of their vital nutrients and live enzymes. Plus, using raw spiralized pasta in a dish will yield a greater number of servings. Of course, you can also cook spiralized pasta. It will be ready in a fraction of the time it typically takes to cook grain-based pasta, usually under five minutes. Simply steam, microwave, simmer in boiling liquid (such as water or broth), pan-fry in oil, deep-fry, bake, or roast it in the oven.

People with hearty appetites will be glad to know that you can eat a larger-sized portion of vegetable or fruit pasta than you can of wheat- or grain-based pasta. Current USDA dietary guidelines recommend between one-half and one cup of cooked whole grains or grain-based pasta per serving. Although there currently is no such recommendation for spiralized vegetable pasta or rice, most spiralizer cookbooks suggest a serving size between one and a half and two cups, which is also the standard used for most of the recipes in this book.

In the pages ahead, you'll find more than thirty-five delicious recipes that use spiralized vegetables or fruits in one form or another, and some recipes even feature several different shapes and sizes of noodles or ribbons. You'll find recipes that run the gamut from breakfast to desserts and from simple to slightly more complex. These recipes contain only vegan ingredients, and many of them are suitable for raw foodists as well as anyone following a gluten-free, paleo, or low-carb diet. I hope that these recipes spark your culinary creativity and encourage you to experiment on your own with using spiralized ingredients in your favorite recipes. Have fun and spiralize with abandonment!

breakfasts, snacks, and sweets

Southwestern-Style Tofu Scramble

This tofu-based vegan version of scrambled eggs, generously spiced with chili powder and other seasonings, was inspired by the cuisine of the American Southwest. It's enhanced with sweet potato, onion, bell pepper, jalapeño chile, black beans, cilantro, and crumbled tortilla chips. Enjoy it as a straightforward scramble or as a filling for breakfast burritos or sandwiches.

1 pound **firm or extra-firm tofu**

2 tablespoons **nutritional yeast flakes**

1 tablespoon **reduced-sodium tamari**

1 tablespoon **chili powder**

1 teaspoon **garlic powder**

1 teaspoon **dried oregano**

½ teaspoon **ground turmeric**

1 large **sweet potato**, peeled

⅔ cup diced **red onion**

⅔ cup diced **red bell pepper**

1 **jalapeño chile**, seeded and finely diced

1 tablespoon **olive oil**

1 cup broken **tortilla chips**

¾ cup cooked **black beans**

¼ cup chopped **fresh cilantro**, lightly packed

Sea salt

Freshly ground black pepper

Crumble the tofu into a small bowl using your fingers. Add the nutritional yeast, tamari, chili powder, garlic powder, oregano, and turmeric and stir until well combined.

Use a tri-blade spiralizer, vertical spiral slicer, or handheld hourglass spiral slicer to cut the sweet potato into thin spaghetti strands, then cut with a knife into 2-inch lengths.

Put the sweet potato, onion, bell pepper, chile, and oil in a large cast iron or nonstick skillet and cook over medium-high heat, stirring occasionally, for 5 minutes. Add the tofu mixture and cook, stirring occasionally, until the vegetables are tender, 8 to 10 minutes. Add the tortilla chips, beans, and cilantro and stir until well combined. Season with salt and pepper to taste. Serve hot.

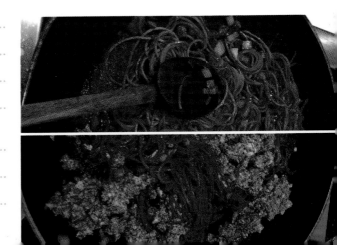

Swiss Chard and Squash Chickpea Frittata

A frittata is an Italian dish that's similar to a crustless quiche, but it frequently contains leftover cooked pasta. This egg-free version is made with a chickpea-flour base that's combined with a blend of Swiss chard, olives, and yellow squash. Enjoy slices for breakfast, as a snack, or with a side salad for a light lunch or dinner.

1 **yellow squash**

1 tablespoon **olive oil**

2½ cups finely chopped **Swiss chard** stems and leaves, lightly packed

1½ tablespoons minced **garlic**

⅓ cup sliced **black or green olives**

¼ cup chopped **fresh basil or Italian parsley**, lightly packed

2 cups **chickpea flour**

2 tablespoons **nutritional yeast flakes**

1½ teaspoons **Italian seasoning**, or ½ teaspoon dried oregano, ½ teaspoon dried thyme, and ½ teaspoon dried rosemary

¾ teaspoon **sea salt**

½ teaspoon **freshly ground black pepper**

½ teaspoon **ground cumin**

½ teaspoon **sweet or smoked paprika**

2 cups **water**

Preheat the oven to 400 degrees F.

Use a tri-blade spiralizer, vertical spiral slicer, or handheld hourglass spiral slicer to cut the squash into thin spaghetti strands, then coarsely chop with a knife into 3-inch lengths.

Put the squash and oil in a 10-inch cast iron or nonstick skillet and cook over medium-high heat, stirring occasionally, for 2 minutes. Add the Swiss chard and garlic and cook, stirring occasionally, for 2 minutes. Add the olives and basil and stir until well combined. Remove from the heat but don't remove the vegetables from the skillet.

Put the chickpea flour, nutritional yeast, Italian seasoning, salt, pepper, cumin, and paprika in a large bowl and whisk until well combined. Add the water and whisk until smooth.

If using a cast iron skillet, add the chickpea mixture and stir to combine with the vegetables. If using a nonstick skillet, oil a 9-inch round or square baking pan. Stir the squash mixture into the chickpea mixture, then pour into the prepared baking pan.

Bake for 30 to 35 minutes, or until the filling is set and slightly firm to the touch. Let cool for 5 minutes. Just before serving, loosen the sides with a knife or thin spatula and cut into 8 pieces. Serve warm, cold, or room temperature.

Fruit-Filled Oat Waffles

YIELD: 4 WAFFLES

These gluten-free waffles are so easy to prepare. Use a blender to first transform the rolled oats into flour, and then use the blender to make the batter. Serve the waffles with maple syrup or your favorite toppings.

1⅓ cups **old-fashioned rolled oats**

1⅓ cups **nondairy milk**

2 tablespoons **cider vinegar**

1 tablespoon **coconut sugar or unbleached cane sugar**

2 teaspoons **vanilla extract**

1 teaspoon **ground cinnamon**

1 teaspoon aluminum-free **baking powder**

½ teaspoon **baking soda**

½ teaspoon **sea salt**

2 **apples, pears, or Asian pears,** peeled

Put the oats in a blender and process into a powdery flour. Add the milk, vinegar, sugar, vanilla extract, cinnamon, baking powder, baking soda, and salt and process until smooth, stopping once to scrape down the blender jar. Transfer to a large bowl.

Use a tri-blade spiralizer or vertical spiral slicer to cut the apples into thin spaghetti strands (see tip), then coarsely chop with a knife into 1-inch lengths. Add the apples to the batter and stir until well combined.

Preheat a waffle iron according to the manufacturer's instructions. When the waffle iron is hot, lightly oil it or mist it with cooking spray. Ladle ¾ cup of the batter onto the iron and cook according to the manufacturer's instructions or until golden brown. Cook the remaining waffles in the same fashion, lightly oiling the waffle iron between each one.

TIP: If using a tri-blade spiralizer, don't core the apples first, as this is accomplished by centering the top end on the small circular corer on the blade plate. Simply remove and discard the seeds after spiralizing. If using a vertical spiral slicer, core the apples prior to spiralizing.

19

Potato Pancakes

Chopped potato strands and onion are pan-fried until golden brown and crispy in this egg-free, gluten-free version of potato pancakes. Serve them plain or topped with applesauce or vegan sour cream.

6 tablespoons **water**

2 teaspoons **chia seeds,** or
2 tablespoons **ground flaxseeds**

1 pound **russet potatoes (2 large),** peeled

½ small **yellow or red onion**

½ cup **brown rice flour**

1½ tablespoons **nutritional yeast flakes**

1 teaspoon **garlic powder**

1 teaspoon **sea salt**

½ teaspoon **sweet or smoked paprika**

½ teaspoon **freshly ground black pepper**

1 tablespoon **olive oil,** or cooking spray as needed

Put the water and chia seeds in a small bowl and whisk until well combined. Set aside for 10 minutes to thicken. Whisk again to break up any clumps of chia seeds.

Use a tri-blade spiralizer or vertical spiral slicer to cut the potatoes and onion into thin spaghetti strands, then coarsely chop with a knife into 2-inch lengths. Transfer to a large bowl. Add the chia seed mixture, flour, nutritional yeast, garlic powder, salt, paprika, and pepper and stir until well combined.

Cook the pancakes in two batches. Put ½ tablespoon of the oil in a large cast iron or nonstick skillet or mist with cooking spray. Heat over medium-high heat. When the skillet is hot, use a ¼-cup measuring cup to portion each pancake and then put it into the hot skillet. Slightly flatten each pancake with a spatula.

Cook until golden brown and crispy on the bottom, 3 to 5 minutes. Flip with a spatula and cook until golden brown and crispy on the other side, 3 to 5 minutes longer. Repeat the process with the remaining oil and potato mixture. Serve immediately.

VARIATION: Replace the potatoes with 1 pound of other peeled and spiralized vegetables, such as beets, carrots, rutabagas, sweet potatoes, turnips, yellow squash, or zucchini. Use a single vegetable or a combination.

Tater-Wrapped Vegan Sausages

Spiralized potatoes are wrapped around vegan sausage links, lightly seasoned, and then baked until golden brown and crispy. The end result is two great tastes in one bite! Serve the sausages for breakfast or a quick snack, plain or with your favorite condiments.

2 large russet potatoes or sweet potatoes, peeled

1 package (8 ounces) vegan breakfast sausage links

Chili powder

Garlic powder

Sea salt

Freshly ground black pepper

Preheat the oven to 425 degrees F. Line a baking sheet with parchment paper or a silicone baking mat.

Use a tri-blade spiralizer, vertical spiral slicer, or handheld hourglass spiral slicer to cut the potatoes into thin spaghetti strands.

For each sausage, use 3 long potato strands. Starting one-half inch from the end of a sausage, wrap the strands around the sausage, overlapping the ends of the strands. Continue wrapping around the entire length of the sausage. Put on the prepared baking sheet and repeat with the remaining sausages.

Lightly oil the wrapped sausages or mist with cooking spray. Sprinkle with chili powder, garlic powder, salt, and pepper as desired. Reposition the sausages as needed to ensure the ends of the potato strands are tucked underneath.

Bake for 20 minutes. Flip the sausages over with a spatula. Bake for 10 to 15 minutes longer, until the potato strands are golden brown and crispy.

Baked Veggie Chips

YIELD: 3 CUPS

Ditch that bag of greasy chips. Instead, use a spiralizer or spiral slicer to make a batch of homemade potato chips or veggie chips from your favorite root vegetables. Season the slices any way you like and then bake them until light and crispy. Now you can snack with abandon!

1 pound **potatoes or root vegetables** (such as sweet potatoes, beets, rutabagas, or parsnips), peeled

2 teaspoons **olive oil**, or cooking spray as needed

Dried herbs (such as Italian seasoning, basil, dill, oregano, thyme, or rosemary)

Ground spices (such as chili powder, curry powder, garlic powder, ground cumin, or paprika)

Sea salt

Freshly ground black pepper

Preheat the oven to 375 degrees F. Line two baking sheets with parchment paper or silicone baking mats.

If using a tri-blade spiralizer, first use a knife to cut a lengthwise slit all the way down one side of each potato. Be sure not to cut the potato all the way through; the knife should reach no farther than the center of the potato. Then spiralize the potatoes into thin slices. Alternatively, use a vertical spiral slicer or handheld hourglass spiral slicer to cut the potatoes into thin ribbons, then tear the ribbons into 2½-inch lengths.

If using oil, transfer the potatoes to a large bowl, add the oil, and toss until evenly coated. Arrange the potatoes in a single layer on the prepared baking sheets. Alternatively, arrange the potatoes in a single layer on the baking sheets and mist with cooking spray. Sprinkle with herbs, spices, salt, and pepper as desired.

Bake the ribbons for 5 minutes or the slices for 10 minutes. Rotate the baking sheets and bake the ribbons for 3 to 5 minutes longer or the slices for 8 to 10 minutes longer, until crisp and lightly browned around the edges.

Maple-Spiced Sweet Potatoes

YIELD: 2 SERVINGS

Cooking sweet potato spaghetti in water keeps this dish low in fat, while the addition of maple syrup and spices elevates the flavor and brings out the natural sweetness of this beloved vegetable. Enjoy this dish plain or with a generous dollop of non-dairy yogurt. It also makes a terrific topping for toast, bagels, pancakes, waffles, or hot cereal.

1 pound **sweet potatoes** (2 large or 3 medium), scrubbed

1 cup frozen **cranberries**, or ⅓ cup dried cranberries

⅔ cup **water**

⅓ cup **toasted chopped pecans**

2 tablespoons **maple syrup**

2 teaspoons **nonhydrogenated margarine or coconut oil** (optional)

1 teaspoon **ground cinnamon**

½ teaspoon **ground ginger**

Sea salt

Use a tri-blade spiralizer, vertical spiral slicer, or handheld hourglass spiral slicer to cut the sweet potatoes into thin spaghetti strands. For easier eating, cut with a knife into 2-inch lengths.

Put the sweet potato, cranberries, and water in a large cast iron or nonstick skillet, cover, and cook over medium-high heat, stirring occasionally, until tender, 8 to 10 minutes. Add the pecans, maple syrup, optional margarine, cinnamon, and ginger and stir until well combined. Season with salt to taste. Serve hot or warm.

Carrot Cake Muffins

YIELD: 12 MUFFINS

These oil- and gluten-free muffins taste like tiny carrot cakes. Their compelling flavor is achieved with an aromatic blend of spices, walnuts, raisins, and carrots. Enjoy the muffins for breakfast or an afternoon snack. For an indulgent dessert, top them with your favorite frosting.

2 large **carrots**, scrubbed or peeled

3 cups **old-fashioned rolled oats**

1½ tablespoons **ground flaxseeds**

1½ teaspoons **baking powder**

1½ teaspoons **ground cinnamon**

1 teaspoon **ground ginger**

¾ teaspoon **baking soda**

½ teaspoon **freshly ground nutmeg**

½ teaspoon **sea salt**

1 cup **nondairy milk**

⅔ cup **agave nectar**

⅔ cup **applesauce**

1 teaspoon **vanilla extract**

½ cup chopped **walnuts**

½ cup **raisins**

Preheat the oven to 400 degrees F. Lightly oil twelve standard muffin cups or mist them with cooking spray. Alternatively, line them with paper liners or use silicone muffin cups.

Use a tri-blade spiralizer, vertical spiral slicer, or handheld hourglass spiral slicer to cut the carrots into thin spaghetti strands, then cut with a knife into 1-inch lengths.

Put the oats in a food processor and process into a powdery flour. Transfer the oat flour to a large bowl. Add the flaxseeds, baking powder, cinnamon, ginger, baking soda, nutmeg, and salt and whisk until well combined. Add the milk, agave nectar, applesauce, and vanilla extract and whisk until well combined. Gently stir in the carrots, walnuts, and raisins.

Fill the prepared muffin cups using a ¼-cup ice-cream scoop or until three-quarters full. Bake for 18 to 20 minutes, or until a toothpick inserted in the center of a muffin comes out clean. Let the muffins cool in the pan for 5 minutes, then transfer them to a rack to finish cooling. Serve warm or room temperature.

Raw Caramel Apple Delight

YIELD: 2 SERVINGS

A mixture of dates, coconut oil, and vanilla extract are blended to create a caramel-like sauce used to top crisp apple spaghetti. The flavor of this dish is reminiscent of a caramel apple. Enjoy it as a light breakfast, a sweet treat during the day, or a satisfying dessert.

¼ cup pitted **soft dates**, soaked for 30 minutes and drained

½ cup **water**

1 teaspoon **coconut oil**, melted

1 teaspoon **vanilla extract**

¼ teaspoon **sea salt**

2 large **apples**, peeled if desired

Ground cinnamon, for garnish

Put the dates, water, oil, vanilla extract, and salt in a blender and process until completely smooth, 1 to 2 minutes.

Use a tri-blade spiralizer or vertical spiral slicer to cut the apples into thin spaghetti strands (see tip, page 19). Leave the strands intact, or for easier eating, cut with a knife into 3-inch lengths.

Arrange the apple on two plates. Drizzle the date mixture over the apples and sprinkle with cinnamon.

VARIATION: Replace the apples with 2 large pears or Asian pears.

25

Pear and Cranberry Crisp

Chopped ribbons of pears are combined with tart cranberries, covered with a sweet-ened and spiced oat-based topping, and oven-baked to perfection. Enjoy the crisp plain or topped with a generous dollop of nondairy yogurt for breakfast. Or try serving it with a scoop of nondairy ice cream for a sweet treat or dessert.

3 **pears**, peeled and stem trimmed

1 cup fresh or frozen **cranberries**

½ cup **turbinado sugar** or **unbleached cane sugar**

1¼ cups **old-fashioned rolled oats**

¾ teaspoon **ground cinnamon**

⅓ cup **nonhydrogenated vegan margarine**

Preheat the oven to 375 degrees F.

Use a tri-blade spiralizer or vertical spiral slicer to cut the pears into thin ribbons (see tip), then coarsely chop with a knife into 2-inch lengths.

Put the pears, cranberries, and ¼ cup of the sugar into a 9-inch square baking pan and stir until well combined.

Put ¼ cup of the rolled oats in a food processor and process into a powdery flour. Transfer the oat flour to a medium bowl. Add the remaining 1 cup of rolled oats, remaining ¼ cup of sugar, and the cinnamon and stir until well combined. Using your fingers, work the margarine into the dry ingredients until the mixture resembles coarse crumbs. Sprinkle evenly over the pear mixture.

Bake for 30 to 35 minutes, or until golden brown and the pears are tender. Let the crisp cool slightly before serving.

TIP: To easily cut the pears into ribbons, use very firm and slightly underripe pears. If using a tri-blade spiralizer, don't core the pears first, as this is accomplished by centering the top end to the small circular corer on the blade plate. Simply remove and discard the seeds after spiralizing. If using, a vertical spiral slicer, core the pears prior to spiralizing.

VARIATION: Replace the pears with 3 peeled Asian pears or apples.

soups, salads, and sides

Miso Soup with Daikon Ramen Noodles

Daikon radish is a commonly used ingredient in Asian cuisine, especially in stir-fries and soups. In this quick-cooking soup, daikon is used as a substitute for ramen noodles and briefly simmered in a miso broth enriched with smoked tofu, edamame, bok choy, and shiitake mushrooms.

½ **white daikon radish**, or
1 **purple daikon radish**, peeled

1 cup thinly sliced **shiitake mushrooms**

1 tablespoon minced **garlic**

1 tablespoon peeled and grated **fresh ginger**

1½ teaspoons **toasted sesame oil**

4 cups **water**

2 heads **baby bok choy**, cut into 1-inch strips

1 cup fresh or frozen **edamame**

1 package (6 ounces) **smoked tofu**, cut into 1-inch strips

½ cup thinly sliced **green onions**

¼ cup **miso**

Sesame seeds, for garnish

Crushed red pepper flakes, for garnish

Use a tri-blade spiralizer or vertical spiral slicer to cut the daikon radish into thin spaghetti strands, then cut with a knife into 4-inch lengths.

Put the mushrooms, garlic, ginger, and oil in a large soup pot and cook over medium-high heat, stirring occasionally, for 2 minutes. Add the water, bok choy, edamame, and tofu and stir to combine. Bring to a boil over high heat. Decrease the heat to low and simmer for 3 minutes.

Add the radish and green onions and simmer until the vegetables are tender, 2 to 3 minutes. Put the miso and ¼ cup of the soup broth in a small bowl and stir until well combined. Add the miso mixture to the soup and stir until well combined. Garnish each serving with sesame seeds and red pepper flakes. Serve immediately.

MISO SOUP WITH CUCUMBER RAMEN NOODLES:
Omit the daikon radish. Use a tri-blade spiralizer or vertical spiral slicer to cut 1 peeled English cucumber or 2 peeled regular cucumbers into thin spaghetti strands, then cut with a knife into 4-inch lengths. Stir into the soup just before serving.

Golden Vegetable Noodle Soup

A combination of nutritional yeast flakes and turmeric is used to create the golden-yellow hue of this vegan version of chicken noodle soup. Spiralized yellow squash works beautifully as a stand-in for traditional wheat noodles.

1 large **yellow squash or zucchini**

1½ cups diced **yellow onion**

1½ cups thinly sliced **carrots**

1½ cups thinly sliced **celery**

1½ tablespoons minced **garlic**

1 tablespoon **olive oil**

4 cups no-salt-added **vegetable broth**

1½ teaspoons **dried thyme**

1 teaspoon **poultry seasoning**

3 tablespoons **nutritional yeast flakes**

3 tablespoons **water**

¼ teaspoon **ground turmeric**

⅓ cup chopped **fresh Italian parsley**, lightly packed

Sea salt

Freshly ground black pepper

Use a tri-blade spiralizer, vertical spiral slicer, or handheld hourglass spiral slicer to cut the squash into thin spaghetti strands, then cut with a knife into 4-inch lengths.

Put the onion, carrots, celery, garlic, and oil in a large soup pot and cook over medium-high heat, stirring occasionally, for 3 minutes. Add the broth, thyme, and poultry seasoning and stir to combine. Bring to a boil over high heat. Cover, decrease the heat to low, and simmer for 10 minutes. Add the squash, cover, and simmer until just tender, 8 to 10 minutes.

Put the nutritional yeast, water, and turmeric in a small bowl and stir until well combined. Add to the soup and stir until well combined. Season with salt and pepper to taste. Serve immediately.

Winter Minestrone

When the weather turns cold, this hearty Italian soup is the ideal choice for a filling lunch or dinner. It's made with a blend of beans, crushed tomatoes, fresh and frozen vegetables, and bite-sized pieces of zucchini and turnip pasta.

1 **turnip** or small **rutabaga**, peeled

1 **zucchini**

1 can (28 ounces) **crushed tomatoes**

3 cups no-salt-added **vegetable broth**

1 can (15 ounces) **mixed beans**, drained and rinsed

1 package (10 ounces) **frozen mixed vegetables** (carrots, corn, green beans, and peas)

3 cups stemmed and coarsely **chopped kale**, lightly packed

1 cup diced **yellow onion**

1 cup diced **celery**

1½ tablespoons minced **garlic**

1 tablespoon **Italian seasoning**

⅓ cup chopped **fresh Italian parsley**, lightly packed

1½ tablespoons **nutritional yeast flakes**

Sea salt

Freshly ground black pepper

Use a tri-blade spiralizer, vertical spiral slicer, or handheld hourglass spiral slicer to cut the turnip and zucchini into thick spaghetti strands, then cut with a knife into 2-inch lengths.

Put the tomatoes, broth, beans, mixed vegetables, kale, onion, celery, and garlic in a large soup pot and stir until well combined. Bring to a boil over high heat. Cover, decrease the heat to low, and simmer for 15 minutes.

Add the turnip and zucchini, cover, and simmer until just tender, 8 to 10 minutes. Add the parsley and nutritional yeast and stir until well combined. Season with salt and pepper to taste. Serve immediately.

Tzatziki-Style Cucumbers

YIELD: 4 SERVINGS

Thin cucumber ribbons are combined with creamy nondairy yogurt, herbs, and lemon juice and zest to create this light, refreshing salad. It's an excellent choice to serve alongside Greek or Middle Eastern dishes, curries, or spicy food of any kind.

1 **English cucumber**, or 2 regular cucumbers

1 cup **plain nondairy yogurt**

Zest and juice of 1 **lemon** (1 to 1½ tablespoons zest and 3 to 4 tablespoons juice)

1½ tablespoons chopped **fresh dill**, or 1½ teaspoons dried dill weed

1½ tablespoons chopped **fresh mint or parsley**

1 tablespoon minced **garlic**

Sea salt

Freshly ground black pepper

Crushed **red pepper flakes or paprika**, for garnish

Use a tri-blade spiralizer, vertical spiral slicer, or handheld hourglass spiral slicer to cut the cucumber into thin ribbons. For easier eating, cut with a knife into 3-inch lengths. Put the cucumber between two paper towels and pat gently to remove excess moisture.

Put the yogurt, lemon zest and juice, dill, mint, and garlic in a large bowl and stir until well combined. Add the cucumber and gently stir to combine. Season with salt and pepper to taste and stir again. Serve immediately or chill for 30 minutes or longer to allow the flavors to blend. Garnish with crushed red pepper flakes or paprika.

TZATZIKI DIP: Cut the cucumber into thin spaghetti strands, then coarsely chop into small pieces with a knife. Proceed with the recipe as directed. Serve with assorted raw veggies, pita bread, or crackers.

Cucumber Noodle Greek Salad

YIELD: 4 SERVINGS

Small cubes of tofu are briefly marinated in a tangy vinaigrette, transforming them into a veganized version of feta cheese. They are then combined with cucumber noodles, bell pepper, cherry tomatoes, red onion, and olives in this modernized version of a classic Greek salad.

2 tablespoons **olive oil**

Zest and juice of ½ **lemon**
(1 to 1½ teaspoons zest and
1½ to 2 tablespoons juice)

1 tablespoon **red wine vinegar**

1 teaspoon minced **garlic**

1 teaspoon **dried oregano**

½ teaspoon **sea salt**

8 ounces **firm or extra-firm tofu,**
cut into ¼-inch cubes, or 1 cup
cooked chickpeas

1 **English cucumber,** or 2 regular
cucumbers

1 small **red onion**

1 cup diced **green bell pepper**

1 cup halved **cherry tomatoes**

⅔ cup pitted **kalamata olives,**
halved

Put the oil, lemon zest and juice, vinegar, garlic, oregano, and salt in a small bowl and whisk until well combined. Add the tofu and gently stir to evenly coat all sides. Refrigerate for 20 minutes.

Use a tri-blade spiralizer, vertical spiral slicer, or handheld hourglass spiral slicer to cut the cucumber into thick spaghetti strands. For easier eating, cut with a knife into 3-inch lengths. Put the cucumber between two paper towels and pat gently to remove excess moisture.

Spiralize the onion into thick spaghetti strands, then cut with a knife into 1½-inch lengths.

Put the cucumber and onion in a large bowl. Add the bell pepper, tomatoes, olives, and tofu mixture and gently toss. Serve immediately or chill for 30 minutes or longer to allow the flavors to blend.

Beet, Carrot, and Orange Salad

This sweet, crisp, and refreshing salad is made with a delightful blend of beet and carrot spaghetti and orange segments tossed in a zesty, ginger-infused vinaigrette.

1 large **red or gold beet**, peeled

2 **carrots**, scrubbed or peeled

2 **oranges**, peeled, seeded, and segmented

¼ cup chopped **fresh parsley**, lightly packed

2 tablespoons **cider vinegar**

1½ tablespoons peeled and grated **fresh ginger**

1 tablespoon **olive oil**

¾ teaspoon **ground cinnamon** (optional)

½ teaspoon **sea salt**

¼ teaspoon **freshly ground black pepper**

Use a tri-blade spiralizer, vertical spiral slicer, or handheld hourglass spiral slicer to cut the beet and carrots into thin spaghetti strands. Leave the strands intact, or for easier eating, cut with a knife into 2½-inch lengths.

Transfer the beet and carrots to a large bowl. Add the oranges and parsley and stir until well combined.

Put the vinegar, ginger, oil, optional cinnamon, salt, and pepper in a small bowl and whisk until well combined. Pour over the beet mixture and toss gently to combine.

VARIATION: For a heartier salad, add 4 cups of baby spinach or coarsely chopped kale, lightly packed, and toss well to combine.

Creamy Coleslaw

You can use a tri-blade spiralizer to quickly shred cabbage for use in salads, slaws, or cooked dishes. This deli-style coleslaw is made with a combination of green and red cabbage and carrots and is dressed with a tangy mayo-based dressing. Serve it as a side salad or use it as part of a crunchy filling for wraps or sandwiches.

1 small **green cabbage, cored**

1 small **red cabbage, cored**

2 **carrots**, scrubbed or peeled

⅓ cup chopped **fresh parsley,** lightly packed

¼ cup thinly sliced **green onion**

¾ cup **vegan mayonnaise**

¼ cup **cider vinegar**

2 tablespoons **spicy brown mustard or Dijon mustard**

1½ tablespoons **agave nectar**

2 teaspoons **whole celery seeds**

1 teaspoon **sea salt**

½ teaspoon **freshly ground black pepper**

Use a tri-blade spiralizer with the straight blade to shred the green and red cabbages by centering the core end on the small circular corer on the blade plate. Measure out 3 cups of each type of cabbage and save the remaining cabbage for another recipe. Switch to the fine shredder blade. Cut the carrots into thin spaghetti strands and coarsely chop with a knife.

Transfer the spiralized cabbages and carrots to a large bowl. Add the parsley and green onion and toss to combine.

Put the mayonnaise, vinegar, mustard, agave nectar, celery seeds, salt, and pepper in a small bowl and whisk until well combined. Pour over the cabbage mixture and stir gently until the vegetables are evenly coated. Serve immediately or refrigerate for 30 minutes to allow the flavors to blend.

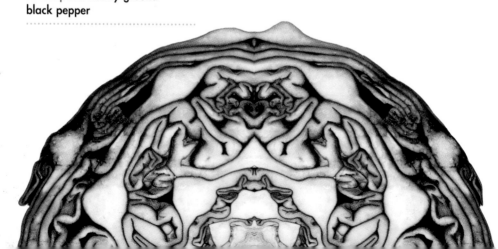

Mixed Greens with Jicama and Apple

YIELD: 4 SERVINGS

The sweet flavor and crisp texture of jicama and apple are complemented by a combination of mixed greens, tart dried cranberries, chopped pecans, and an apple-mustard vinaigrette in this autumn-inspired salad.

1 large **Granny Smith or other apple**

¼ **jicama, peeled**

¼ cup **cider vinegar**

1 tablespoon **olive oil**

1 tablespoon **spicy brown mustard or stone-ground mustard**

1 tablespoon **agave nectar**

1 tablespoon peeled and grated **fresh ginger**

3 ounces (about 4 cups) **mixed baby greens**

⅓ cup dried **cranberries or goji berries**

⅓ cup chopped **raw or toasted pecans**

Use a tri-blade spiralizer or vertical spiral slicer to cut the apple into thin spaghetti strands (see tip, page 19), then coarsely chop with a knife into 2½-inch lengths. Set aside the leftover scraps from spiralizing the apple. Spiralize the jicama into thin spaghetti strands, then cut with a knife into 2½-inch lengths.

To make the dressing, put the apple scraps, vinegar, oil, mustard, agave nectar, and ginger in a blender and process until smooth, stopping once to scrape down the blender jar.

Put the greens, spiralized apple and jicama, cranberries, and pecans in a large bowl and toss gently. Add the dressing and toss gently until evenly distributed. Serve immediately.

Psychedelic Salad

YIELD: 6 SERVINGS

This multitextured and visually stunning salad will delight the senses. The colorful combination consists of rainbow Swiss chard, red kale, maroon carrots, gold beet, red cabbage, watermelon radish, and striped chioggia beet. After preparation, the vegetables are tossed with a sweet-and-tangy citrus vinaigrette that unifies the ingredients without overpowering them.

2 **maroon carrots**, scrubbed or peeled

1 **gold beet**, peeled

1 **chioggia beet**, peeled

1 **watermelon radish**, peeled

½ small **red cabbage**, cored

3 leaves **rainbow Swiss chard**, stems and leaves thinly sliced

2 leaves **red kale**, stemmed and thinly sliced

Zest and juice of 1 **orange** (2 tablespoons zest and ⅓ cup juice)

¼ cup chopped **fresh Italian parsley**, lightly packed

3 tablespoons **olive oil**

1½ tablespoons **stone-ground mustard**

1½ tablespoons **agave nectar**

½ teaspoon **sea salt**

½ teaspoon **freshly ground black pepper**

¼ cup **hemp seeds**

Use a tri-blade spiralizer to cut the carrots and gold beet into thin spaghetti strands, then cut with a knife into 2½-inch lengths. Switch to the straight blade and cut the chioggia beet and watermelon radish into thin ribbons, then cut with a knife into 2½-inch lengths. Use the same blade to shred the cabbage by centering the core end on the small circular corer on the blade plate. Measure out 1½ cups of cabbage and save the remaining cabbage for another recipe.

Put the Swiss chard, kale, carrots, gold beet, chioggia beet, radish, and cabbage in a large bowl and toss gently.

Put the orange zest and juice, parsley, oil, mustard, agave nectar, salt, and pepper in a small bowl and whisk until well combined. Pour over the vegetables and toss gently. Sprinkle with the hemp seeds. Serve immediately.

TIP: If you don't have a tri-blade spiralizer, you can still make this salad. Use a vertical spiral slicer or handheld hourglass spiral slicer (depending on the model) to cut the carrots, both beets, and the radish as described above. Then cut the red cabbage into thin strips with a knife.

Baked Curly Fries

Eating too many deep-fried French fries can add inches to your waistline. But you can satisfy your craving for fries without the guilt by oven-baking spiralized potatoes or your favorite root vegetables. Enjoy them as a side dish or snack.

1 pound **potatoes or root vegetables** (such as beets, kohlrabi, parsnips, rutabagas, or sweet potatoes), peeled

1½ tablespoons **olive oil, or cooking spray** as needed

1½ tablespoons **nutritional yeast flakes**

1 tablespoon **garlic powder**

1½ teaspoons **dried herbs** (such as basil, dill, Italian seasoning, oregano, rosemary, or thyme)

Sea salt

Freshly ground black pepper

Preheat the oven to 450 degrees F. Line a baking sheet with parchment paper or a silicone baking mat.

Use a tri-blade spiralizer, vertical spiral slicer, or handheld hourglass spiral slicer to cut the potatoes into thick spaghetti strands. For easier eating, cut with a knife into 4-inch lengths.

If using oil, transfer the potatoes to a large bowl, add the oil, nutritional yeast, garlic powder, and dried herbs, and toss until evenly coated. Arrange the potatoes in a single layer on the prepared baking sheet. Alternatively, put the potatoes on the baking sheet, sprinkle them with the nutritional yeast, garlic powder, and dried herbs, and toss until evenly coated. Spread into a single layer and mist with cooking spray. Sprinkle with salt and pepper as desired.

Bake for 15 minutes. Flip with a spatula and spread back into a single layer. Bake for 10 to 15 minutes longer, until crisp and lightly browned around the edges.

BAKED SHOESTRING FRIES: Spiralize the potatoes or root vegetables into thin spaghetti strands, decrease the oven temperature to 425 degrees F, and proceed as directed.

Quinoa and Root Vegetable Pilaf

YIELD: 6 SERVINGS

Celeriac and kohlrabi might be two of the strangest-looking vegetables you'll ever see, but they're quite delicious and taste a lot like their close cousins, celery and broccoli respectively. This pilaf recipe showcases their versatility, as rice-sized pieces of each vegetable are cooked along with tricolor quinoa, spinach, and sliced almonds.

1 **celeriac**, peeled

2 **kohlrabi**, peeled

1½ tablespoons minced **garlic**

1 tablespoon **toasted sesame oil**

1 cup **tricolor quinoa**, rinsed

3 tablespoons chopped **fresh thyme**, or 1 tablespoon dried

2 cups no-salt-added **vegetable broth**

1 package (5 ounces) **baby spinach**

½ cup thinly sliced **green onions**

⅓ cup chopped **fresh Italian parsley**

⅓ cup **toasted sliced almonds**

2 tablespoons **nutritional yeast flakes**

Sea salt

Freshly ground black pepper

Use a tri-blade spiralizer or vertical spiral slicer to cut the celeriac and kohlrabi into thin spaghetti strands. Transfer to a food processor and pulse into rice-sized pieces.

Put the celeriac mixture, garlic, and oil in a large saucepan and cook over medium-high heat, stirring occasionally, for 5 minutes. Add the quinoa and thyme and cook, stirring occasionally, for 1 minute. Add the broth and stir to combine. Bring to a boil over high heat. Cover, decrease the heat to low, and cook until the quinoa is tender and all the broth is absorbed, 15 to 18 minutes.

Add the spinach and green onions and cook, stirring occasionally, until the spinach is wilted, 1 to 2 minutes. Add the parsley, almonds, and nutritional yeast and stir until well combined. Season with salt and pepper to taste. Serve hot.

TIP: Use this pilaf as a stuffing for baked vegetables, such as bell peppers or winter squash.

Gold Beet and Vegetable Biryani

YIELD: 4 SERVINGS

Rice is swapped for pulverized strands of gold beets in this fragrant and flavorful Indian-inspired dish. Red bell pepper and peas add a splash of color, and their flavors and textures contrast beautifully with the sweet raisins and crunchy cashews.

1½ pounds **gold beets**, peeled

1 cup diced **yellow onion**

1 **jalapeño chile or small red chile**, seeded and finely diced

1½ tablespoons minced **garlic**

1½ tablespoons peeled and grated **fresh ginger**

1 tablespoon **coconut oil**, melted

1 **red bell pepper**, diced

1 teaspoon **curry powder or garam masala**

1 cup **fresh or thawed frozen peas**

½ cup **toasted cashews**

⅓ cup **raisins**

⅓ cup chopped **fresh cilantro**, lightly packed

Sea salt

Freshly ground black pepper

Use a tri-blade spiralizer, vertical spiral slicer, or handheld hourglass spiral slicer to cut the beets into thin spaghetti strands. Transfer the beets to a food processor and pulse into rice-sized pieces.

Put the beets, onion, chile, garlic, ginger, and oil in a large cast iron or nonstick skillet and cook over medium-high heat, stirring occasionally, for 3 minutes. Add bell pepper and curry powder and cook, stirring occasionally, until the vegetables are tender, about 3 minutes. Add the peas, cashews, raisins, and cilantro and cook, stirring occasionally, for 1 minute. Season with salt and pepper to taste.

main dishes

Hummus and Veggie-Filled Collard Rolls

YIELD: 4 SERVINGS

Large leaves of collard greens replace the standard soft tortillas in these crunchy, taco-style wraps. Loaded with creamy hummus, alfalfa sprouts, and spiralized carrots, cucumber, and jicama, they make a satisfying, wholesome meal.

1 **carrot**, scrubbed or peeled

¼ **English cucumber**, or ½ regular cucumber

¼ **jicama**, peeled

4 large **collard green leaves**, stems trimmed

¾ cup **hummus**

½ cup **alfalfa sprouts**

Use a tri-blade spiralizer, vertical spiral slicer, or handheld hourglass spiral slicer to cut the carrot, cucumber, and jicama into thin spaghetti strands, then cut with a knife into 1½-inch lengths. Measure out 1 cup each of the carrot, cucumber, and jicama and save the remaining for another recipe.

To assemble each roll, put 1 collard leaf flat on a large plate, shiny-side up. Spread 3 tablespoons of the hummus in the center of the leaf. In parallel rows over the hummus, arrange ¼ cup of the spiralized carrot, cucumber, and jicama, and then top with 2 tablespoons of the alfalfa sprouts. Fold in the right side of the collard leaf toward the center over the filling and then fold in and overlap the left side of the leaf. Repeat the process with the remaining collard leaves, hummus, spiralized vegetables, and sprouts. Serve immediately.

VARIATION: Replace the collard green leaves with 4 large leaves of Swiss chard or kale.

Farmers' Market Quesadillas

Spiralized zucchini and yellow squash are combined with onion, bell pepper, corn, and plenty of vegan cheese to make the filling for these quesadillas. Serve them as an entrée or snack topped with salsa, vegan sour cream, and guacamole or diced avocado.

1 large **zucchini**

1 large **yellow squash**

1 small **red onion**, diced

1 **red or orange bell pepper**, diced

1 cup **fresh or frozen corn kernels**

1½ tablespoons **olive oil**

1½ tablespoons minced **garlic**

1 tablespoon **nutritional yeast flakes**

1½ teaspoons **chili powder**

1 teaspoon **dried oregano**

Sea salt

Freshly ground black pepper

6 (8-inch) **tortillas or gluten-free tortillas**

1½ cups shredded **vegan cheddar cheese**

Salsa

Guacamole or diced avocado

Vegan sour cream

Use a tri-blade spiralizer, vertical spiral slicer, or handheld hourglass spiral slicer to cut the zucchini and yellow squash into thin spaghetti strands, then cut with a knife into 2½-inch lengths.

Put the onion, bell pepper, corn, and oil in a large cast iron or nonstick skillet and cook over medium-high heat, stirring occasionally, for 5 minutes. Add the zucchini, yellow squash, and garlic and cook, stirring occasionally, for 5 minutes. Add the nutritional yeast, chili powder, and oregano and stir until well combined. Season with salt and pepper to taste.

To assemble each quesadilla, put 1 tortilla on a large plate. Spoon ½ cup of the vegetable mixture over half the tortilla and top with ¼ cup of the cheese. Fold the tortilla over to enclose the filling. Repeat with the remaining tortillas, vegetable mixture, and cheese.

Lightly oil a skillet or mist with cooking spray and put over medium heat. Cook the quesadillas in batches in the hot skillet until lightly browned on the bottom, 2 to 3 minutes. Flip with a spatula and cook until lightly browned on the other side, 2 to 3 minutes. Garnish with salsa, guacamole, and vegan sour cream.

Lemon-Walnut Parsnip Pasta

YIELD: 3 SERVINGS

The parsnip is a root vegetable that's pale cream in color and has a much sweeter flavor than its carrot cousin. Cooking parsnips very simply with just walnuts and garlic in olive oil and adding a final flourish of lemon accentuates their sweet, earthy flavor.

2 large **parsnips** (about 1½ pounds), peeled

2 tablespoons **olive oil**

½ cup chopped **walnuts**

2 tablespoons minced **garlic**

Zest and juice of 2 **lemons** (3 to 4 tablespoons zest and ⅓ to ½ cup juice)

⅓ cup chopped **fresh parsley,** lightly packed

1½ tablespoons **nutritional yeast flakes**

½ teaspoon **crushed red pepper flakes** (optional)

Sea salt

Freshly ground black pepper

Use a tri-blade spiralizer or handheld hourglass spiral slicer to cut the parsnips into thin spaghetti strands. For easier eating, cut with a knife into 4-inch lengths.

Put the oil in a large cast iron or nonstick pan and heat over medium-high heat. When the oil is hot, add the walnuts and garlic and cook, stirring occasionally, for 2 minutes. Add the parsnips and cook, stirring occasionally, until tender, 3 to 5 minutes.

Add the lemon zest and juice, parsley, nutritional yeast, and red pepper flakes and stir until well combined. Season with salt and pepper to taste.

LEMON-WALNUT RAW ZUCCHINI PASTA: Replace the parsnips with 3 zucchini (about 1½ pounds). Spiralize and cut as directed. Put the zucchini in a large bowl and add 1½ cups of diced bell peppers (a mix of green, red, orange, or yellow) along with the oil, walnuts, garlic, lemon zest and juice, parsley, nutritional yeast, and optional red pepper flakes. Toss to combine. Season with salt and pepper to taste and toss again. Serve immediately.

Noodles with Cashew Alfredo Sauce

YIELD: 4 SERVINGS

Soaked cashews are used in this recipe to create a rich, creamy, vegan version of Alfredo sauce, perfect for coating spiralized vegetable noodles.

1 cup **raw cashew pieces**, soaked for 1 hour and drained

1¼ cups **water**

¼ cup **nutritional yeast flakes**

Zest and juice of 1 **lemon** (1 to 1½ tablespoons zest and 3 to 4 tablespoons juice)

2 large cloves **garlic**

1 teaspoon **sea salt**

½ teaspoon **freshly ground black pepper**

⅛ teaspoon **freshly grated nutmeg**

3 large or 4 medium **zucchini, yellow squash, or peeled medium sweet potatoes or carrots**, or a combination

To make the sauce, put the cashews, water, nutritional yeast, lemon zest and juice, garlic, salt, pepper, and nutmeg in a blender and process until completely smooth, stopping once to scrape down the blender jar. Transfer to a medium saucepan and cook over medium heat, whisking occasionally, until thickened, 3 to 5 minutes. Remove from the heat.

To make the noodles, use a tri-blade spiralizer, vertical spiral slicer, or handheld hourglass spiral slicer to cut the zucchini into thin or thick spaghetti strands. Leave the strands intact, or for easier eating, cut with a knife into 4-inch lengths. Transfer to a large bowl, add the sauce, and toss gently. Serve immediately.

VARIATION: To serve as a cooked pasta dish, steam, microwave, or boil the zucchini or cook it in a skillet with a little oil until tender, 2 to 3 minutes. Transfer to a large bowl, add the sauce, and toss gently. Serve hot. Makes 3 servings.

Fiesta Fettuccine

Love guacamole? Then you'll love this recipe, which uses chunky guacamole to coat thick strands of zucchini and yellow squash. This all-raw recipe requires no cooking, making it ideal for a light yet filling warm-weather dinner.

3 Hass **avocados**

Zest and juice of 2 **limes**
(2 to 3 teaspoons zest and
3 to 4 tablespoons juice)

1½ tablespoons **nutritional yeast flakes**

1½ tablespoons minced **garlic**

¾ cup **fresh or frozen corn kernels**

¾ cup finely diced **tomatoes**

¾ cup finely diced **orange bell pepper**

½ cup finely diced **red onion**

1 **jalapeño chile**, seeded and finely diced

⅓ cup chopped **fresh cilantro**, lightly packed

Sea salt

Freshly ground black pepper

2 **zucchini**

1 **yellow squash**

Put the avocados, lime zest and juice, nutritional yeast, and garlic in a large bowl and mash with a fork until very smooth. Add the corn, tomatoes, bell pepper, onion, chile, and cilantro and stir to combine. Season with salt and pepper to taste.

Use a tri-blade spiralizer, vertical spiral slicer, or handheld hourglass spiral slicer to cut the zucchini and yellow squash into thick spaghetti strands. For easier eating, cut with a knife into 4-inch lengths. Add to the avocado mixture and gently toss. Serve immediately.

49

Seeding and dicing a jalapeño

Raw Pad Thai

YIELD: 4 SERVINGS

Pad Thai is traditionally made with rice noodles, but spiralized zucchini and carrots are a more nutritious and flavorful choice. The fresh vegetable noodles are combined with shredded red cabbage, mung bean sprouts, and pea pods and then tossed with a spicy peanut sauce.

½ cup **peanut butter**

2 tablespoons **reduced-sodium tamari**

2 tablespoons **toasted sesame oil**

Zest and juice of 1 **lime**
(1 to 1½ teaspoons zest and
1½ to 2 tablespoons juice)

1 tablespoon **coconut sugar**

1 tablespoon minced **garlic**

1 tablespoon peeled and grated **fresh ginger**

½ teaspoon **crushed red pepper flakes**

1 large **zucchini**

2 large **carrots**, scrubbed or peeled

¾ cup **mung bean sprouts**

¾ cup **pea pods**, halved crosswise

½ cup shredded **red cabbage**

½ cup thinly sliced **green onions**

⅓ cup chopped **fresh cilantro**, lightly packed

¼ cup chopped **raw or roasted peanuts**

To make the sauce, put the peanut butter, tamari, oil, lime zest and juice, sugar, garlic, ginger, and red pepper flakes in a blender and process until smooth, stopping once to scrape down the blender jar.

To make the noodles, use a tri-blade spiralizer, vertical spiral slicer, or handheld hourglass spiral slicer to cut the zucchini and carrots into thin spaghetti strands, then cut with a knife into 4-inch lengths. Transfer to a large bowl and add the sprouts, pea pods, cabbage, green onions, and cilantro and toss gently. Add the sauce and toss until evenly distributed. Sprinkle with the peanuts. Serve immediately.

VARIATION: For a peanut-free version, replace the peanut butter with another nut or seed butter and replace the chopped peanuts with other chopped nuts or seeds.

Teriyaki Tofu Stir-Fry with Carrot Noodles

YIELD: 4 SERVINGS

Tofu, broccoli, bell pepper, celery, and pineapple are stir-fried, blanketed with a sweet-and-sour teriyaki sauce, and served over spiralized carrot spaghetti. Sweet, savory, and delish!

¼ cup reduced-sodium **tamari**

¼ cup **brown rice vinegar**

3 tablespoons **coconut sugar**

2 tablespoons **toasted sesame oil**

1½ tablespoons minced **garlic**

1½ tablespoons peeled and grated **fresh ginger**

1½ teaspoons **cornstarch**

½ teaspoon **crushed red pepper flakes**

3 large **carrots**, scrubbed or peeled

1 pound **firm tofu**, cut into ½-inch cubes

2 cups small **broccoli florets**

1 **red bell pepper**, diced

2 stalks **celery**, thinly sliced

1 cup **pineapple tidbits or chunks**, drained

½ cup **raw or roasted cashew pieces**

⅓ cup thinly sliced **green onions**

⅓ cup chopped **fresh cilantro**, lightly packed

To make the sauce, put the tamari, vinegar, sugar, 1 tablespoon of the oil, and the garlic, ginger, cornstarch, and red pepper flakes in a small bowl and whisk until well combined.

To make the carrot spaghetti, use a tri-blade spiralizer, vertical spiral slicer, or handheld hourglass spiral slicer to cut the carrots into thin spaghetti strands, then cut with a knife into 4-inch lengths. Use the strands raw or steam or microwave them until tender, 2 to 3 minutes.

To make the stir-fry, put the tofu and remaining tablespoon of oil in a large cast iron or nonstick skillet or wok and cook over medium-high heat, stirring occasionally, until lightly browned on all sides, 8 to 10 minutes. Add the broccoli, bell pepper, celery, and pineapple and cook, stirring occasionally, until the vegetables are crisp-tender, 3 to 5 minutes.

Add the cashews and green onions and cook, stirring occasionally, for 1 minute. Add the sauce and cilantro and cook, stirring constantly, for 1 minute, until the sauce thickens. Serve hot over the carrot spaghetti.

TERIYAKI TOFU STIR-FRY WITH CARROT RICE: Transfer the raw or cooked carrot strands to a food processor and pulse into rice-sized pieces. Serve the stir-fry over the carrot rice.

Pesto Pasta

A combination of basil and parsley are used in this pesto recipe, but it's the addition of lemon juice and zest that makes the flavor really pop. Tossed with zucchini pasta, pesto never had it this good!

1 cup **fresh basil leaves, packed**

½ cup **fresh Italian parsley, packed**

¼ cup **nutritional yeast flakes**

¼ cup **pine nuts or chopped walnuts**

3 tablespoons **olive oil**

Zest and juice of 1 **lemon** (1 to 1½ tablespoons zest and 3 to 4 tablespoons juice)

4 large cloves **garlic**

½ teaspoon **sea salt**

¼ teaspoon **freshly ground black pepper**

3 large or 4 medium **zucchini or yellow squash** or a combination

To make the pesto, put the basil, parsley, nutritional yeast, pine nuts, oil, lemon zest and juice, garlic, salt, and pepper in a food processor and process until completely smooth, 1 to 2 minutes.

To make the zucchini spaghetti, use a tri-blade spiralizer, vertical spiral slicer, or handheld hourglass spiral slicer to cut the zucchini into thin or thick spaghetti strands. Leave the strands intact, or for easier eating, cut with a knife into 4-inch lengths. Transfer to a large bowl, add the pesto, and toss gently. Serve immediately.

VARIATION: To serve as a cooked pasta dish, steam, microwave, or boil the zucchini or cook it in a skillet with a little oil until tender, 2 to 3 minutes. Transfer to a large bowl, add the pesto, and toss gently. Serve hot. Makes 3 servings.

Raw Marinara with Veggie Pasta

A combination of fresh and sun-dried tomatoes, along with plenty of fresh basil and garlic, intensifies the flavor of this rich-tasting marinara sauce. The addition of dates and red bell pepper adds a touch of sweetness and balances the natural acidity of the tomatoes.

⅓ cup **sun-dried tomatoes**

⅓ cup **warm water**

2 pitted **soft dates**

3 cups diced **tomatoes**

1 **red bell pepper,** coarsely chopped

½ cup **fresh basil leaves,** packed

2 tablespoons **olive oil**

1 tablespoon **nutritional yeast flakes**

3 large cloves **garlic**

1 teaspoon **dried oregano**

½ teaspoon **crushed red pepper flakes**

½ teaspoon **sea salt**

¼ teaspoon **freshly ground black pepper**

3 large or 4 medium **zucchini** or **yellow squash** or a combination

To make the marinara sauce, put the sun-dried tomatoes, water, and dates in a small bowl and set aside for 15 minutes to rehydrate the tomatoes. Drain off any excess water. Transfer the sun-dried tomatoes and dates to a food processor. Add the fresh tomatoes, bell pepper, basil, oil, nutritional yeast, garlic, oregano, red pepper flakes, salt, and pepper and process until completely smooth, 2 to 3 minutes.

To make the spaghetti, use a tri-blade spiralizer, vertical spiral slicer, or handheld hourglass spiral slicer to cut the zucchini into thin or thick spaghetti strands. Leave the strands intact, or for easier eating, cut with a knife into 4-inch lengths. Transfer to a large bowl, add the sauce, and toss gently. Serve immediately.

VARIATION: To serve as a cooked pasta dish, steam, microwave, or boil the zucchini or cook it in a skillet with a little oil until tender, 2 to 3 minutes. Transfer to a large bowl, add the sauce, and toss gently. Serve hot. Makes 3 servings.

Tempeh Meatballs with Veggie Spaghetti

YIELD: 4 SERVINGS

Tempeh is blended with onion, garlic, chickpea flour, and a generous amount of seasonings to create a flavorful batch of oven-baked meatless meatballs. The meatballs are then combined with homemade marinara sauce and spiralized vegetable spaghetti to make a hearty, veganized version of this popular Italian dish.

½ small **yellow onion**

4 large cloves **garlic**

8 ounces **tempeh**, broken into large pieces

2 tablespoons **balsamic vinegar**

2 tablespoons reduced-sodium **tamari**

1½ tablespoons **Italian seasoning**

¾ teaspoon **ground fennel**

¾ teaspoon **crushed red pepper flakes**

½ teaspoon **freshly ground black pepper**

½ cup **chickpea flour**

Raw Marinara with Veggie Pasta (page 54), prepared as directed

Preheat the oven to 450 degrees F. Line a baking sheet with parchment paper or a silicone baking mat.

To make the meatballs, put the onion and garlic in a food processor and process until finely chopped, 30 to 45 seconds. Add the tempeh, vinegar, tamari, Italian seasoning, fennel, red pepper flakes, and pepper and process into coarse crumbs, 1 to 2 minutes. Scrape down the container with a silicone spatula. Add the flour and process until well combined.

Using your hands, roll the tempeh mixture into 1½-inch balls. Arrange the balls on the prepared baking sheet and lightly oil them or mist with cooking spray. Bake for 15 minutes. Roll the balls over using a silicone or metal spatula and bake for 10 to 15 minutes longer, until they are dry and golden brown.

While the tempeh meatballs are baking, put the marinara sauce in a large saucepan and cook over medium heat, stirring occasionally, until hot, 2 to 3 minutes. Add the tempeh meatballs, stir gently to coat with the sauce, and cook until heated through, 3 to 4 minutes. Serve immediately over the veggie pasta.

VARIATION: For an easier preparation, replace the Raw Marinara with 3 cups of jarred marinara sauce.

Beet Noodles with Italian Kale and Chickpeas

YIELD: 4 SERVINGS

Beets have an earthy, slightly sweet flavor that is heightened when the beets are cooked with kale, chickpeas, garlic, and herbs. This is a visually stunning and filling dish.

1½ pounds **red, gold, or chioggia beets**, peeled

1 cup diced **yellow or red onion**

1½ tablespoons **olive oil**

1 bunch (1 pound) **Tuscan kale**, stemmed and cut into thin strips

1½ tablespoons minced **garlic**

1½ tablespoons chopped **fresh dill**, or 1½ teaspoons dried dill weed

1½ tablespoons chopped **fresh thyme**, or 1½ teaspoons dried

1 can (15 ounces) **chickpeas**, drained and rinsed

1½ tablespoons **nutritional yeast flakes**

Sea salt

Freshly ground black pepper

Use a tri-blade spiralizer, vertical spiral slicer, or handheld hourglass spiral slicer to cut the beets into thin spaghetti strands. Leave the strands intact, or for easier eating, cut with a knife into 4-inch lengths.

Put the onion and oil in a large cast iron or non-stick skillet and cook over medium-high heat, stirring occasionally, for 3 minutes. Add the kale and garlic and cook, stirring occasionally, for 2 minutes. Add the beets, dill, and thyme and cook, stirring occasionally, until the vegetables are tender, 5 to 7 minutes. Add the chickpeas and nutritional yeast and stir until well combined. Season with salt and pepper to taste. Serve hot.

Stemming and slicing Tuscan kale

Veggie Curry with Butternut Noodles

YIELD: 4 SERVINGS

This mild curry features a vibrant assortment of vegetables, including broccoli, red bell pepper, and butternut squash. The veggies are cloaked in a rich sauce made with a combination of curry paste, vegetable broth, and coconut milk and then combined with thick butternut squash noodles.

1 medium **butternut squash** (2 pounds), peeled

1 small **yellow or red onion**, diced

1 **red bell pepper**, diced

1½ tablespoons minced **garlic**

1½ tablespoons peeled and grated **fresh ginger**

1 tablespoon **coconut oil**, melted

1½ cups no-salt-added **vegetable broth**

3 tablespoons **red or yellow curry paste**

3 cups small **broccoli florets**

1 can (14 ounces) **lite coconut milk**

½ cup **frozen peas**

⅓ cup chopped **fresh cilantro**

Sea salt

Freshly ground black pepper

Cut off the bulbous bottom part of the squash, just above the seed cavity. Remove and discard the seeds, then cut into 1-inch cubes.

Cut the top part of the squash in half lengthwise, then cut a lengthwise slit all the way down one side of each half. Use a tri-blade spiralizer to cut the squash into thick spaghetti strands, then cut with a knife into 4-inch lengths.

Put the onion, bell pepper, garlic, ginger, and oil in a large saucepan and cook over medium-high heat, stirring occasionally, for 3 minutes. Put the broth and curry paste in a small bowl and stir until well combined. Add the broth mixture, squash cubes, and broccoli to the saucepan and stir until well combined. Bring to a boil over high heat. Cover, decrease the heat to low, and cook, stirring occasionally, for 20 minutes.

Add the squash spaghetti, coconut milk, peas, and cilantro and stir until well combined. Cover and cook, stirring occasionally, for 10 to 15 minutes, until the vegetables are tender. Season with salt and pepper to taste. Serve hot.

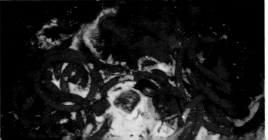

Butternut Squash Mac-n-Cheese

A large butternut squash does double duty in this vegan macaroni-and-cheese recipe. The top part of the squash is used to create the macaroni-shaped pasta, and the bottom part is used to flavor and tint the cheesy-tasting sauce.

1 large **butternut squash** (3 pounds), peeled

1 cup **unsweetened nondairy milk**

½ cup **nutritional yeast flakes**

1 tablespoon **tapioca starch**

1 teaspoon **sea salt**

¾ teaspoon **garlic powder**

¾ teaspoon **onion powder**

¾ teaspoon **sweet or smoked paprika**

½ teaspoon **freshly ground black pepper**

Preheat the oven to 400 degrees F. Line two baking sheets with parchment paper or silicone baking mats.

Cut off the bulbous bottom part of the squash, just above the seed cavity. Remove and discard the seeds, then cut into 1-inch cubes. Arrange the cubes in a single layer on one of the prepared baking sheets.

Cut the top part of the squash in half lengthwise, then cut a lengthwise slit all the way down one side of each half. Use a tri-blade spiralizer to cut the squash into thick spaghetti strands, then cut with a knife into large macaroni-sized lengths. Transfer the squash macaroni to the other prepared baking sheet.

Lightly oil the squash cubes and macaroni or mist with cooking spray. Bake until tender, 10 to 15 minutes.

To make the sauce, transfer the squash cubes to a food processor. Add the milk, nutritional yeast, tapioca starch, salt, garlic powder, onion powder, paprika, and pepper and process until completely smooth, 1 to 2 minutes. Transfer to a large saucepan and cook over medium heat, whisking occasionally, until thickened, 3 to 5 minutes. Remove from the heat, add the squash macaroni, and stir until evenly coated with the sauce. Serve hot.

ABOUT THE AUTHOR

 **Beverly Lynn Bennett** is an experienced vegan chef and baker, writer, and animal advocate who is passionate about showing the world how easy, delicious, and healthy it is to live and eat as a vegan. A certified food-service operations manager, she earned her culinary arts degree in 1988 from the University of Akron, Ohio, and in the following years worked in and managed vegan and vegetarian restaurants and natural food stores.

Vegan since the early 1990s, Beverly is the author of *Vegan Bites: Recipes for Singles, Chia: Using the Ancient Superfood, Kale: The Nutritional Powerhouse,* and *The Complete Idiot's Guide to Vegan Slow Cooking.* She is also the coauthor of *The Complete Idiot's Guide to Vegan Living, The Complete Idiot's Guide to Vegan Cooking,* and *The Complete Idiot's Guide to Gluten-Free Vegan Cooking.* Her work has appeared in many national and international print publications, on public television and DVD, and all over the web. She has hosted the popular Vegan Chef website at VeganChef.com since 1999 and has been a regular columnist for *VegNews* magazine since 2002.

Beverly currently lives and works in Eugene, Oregon, where her love of organic, healthy, and vibrant foods fuels a passion for developing innovative vegan recipes. When she isn't hard at work in the kitchen, she can often be found frequenting farmers' markets and educating others on issues relating to veganism and health through cooking demos and speaking engagements.

© 2015 Beverly Lynn Bennett

Food photography: Alan Roettinger
Book design, photo editing: John Wincek
Editing: Jo Stepaniak

Pictured on front cover: Lemon-Walnut
Raw Zucchini Pasta, page 46

ISBN: 978-1-155312-052-0

Printed in the United States of America

Library of Congress Cataloging-in-Publication Data

Bennett, Beverly Lynn.
  Spiralize! : transform vegetables and fruits from ordinary to extraordinary / Beverly Lynn Bennett.
     pages cm
   ISBN 978-1-55312-052-0 (pbk.)
1. Gluten-free diet.   2. Gluten-free foods.
3. Gluten-free diet—Recipes.   I. Title.
   RM237.86B46 2015
   641.5'63—dc23
                                        2015015869

Published by **Books Alive**
An imprint of Book Publishing Company
PO Box 99
Summertown, TN 38483

931-964-3571
888-260-8458
bookpubco.com

Sources for the spiralizers pictured in this book:

Brieftons InstantVeg, NextGen, and Tri-Blade
brieftons.com

GEFU USA Spiralfix and Spirelli
gefu.us

Paderno World-Cuisine 4-Blade and Tri-Blade
padernousa.com

Our appreciation to these manufacturers for their assistance.

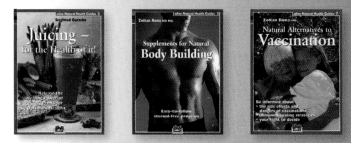